Not What We A

NOT WHAT WE APPEAR TO BE

New Perspectives for Conscious Living

MONTI SCRIBNER

Formulas4Living

Paperback:
ISBN-10: 1-941065-27-9
ISBN-13: 978-1-941065-27-3

eBook:
ISBN-10: 1-941065-28-7
ISBN-13: 978-1-941065-28-0

Gratefully dedicated to my teachers, seen and unseen, who have guided me in the unfolding of this extraordinary journey.

Contents

PREFACE

My Journey

The Ties That Bind

I was the first child and my parents were hoping for a boy. When I asked about my name, they said they were going to name me Monti whether I was a boy or a girl. I later learned that my father married my mother because she was much like his own mother. She was beautiful, self-involved, and emanated anger so palpable I could sense it no matter where she was in the house. My father was silently complacent and rarely expressed himself (no one else in the family did, either) because my mother spoke in a constant stream of consciousness without ever seeming to take a breath.

I grew up in the '50s when relationships, emotions, and questions about the meaning of life weren't generally topics of conversation. Saying I love you, hugging, touching, and affection didn't happen either—at least not so far as I knew. We were never to discuss problems or indicate that we had less than anyone else. We maintained the appearance that we were just like everyone else. As far as the outside world was concerned, we were the picture-perfect family.

The spaces in our house were filled with my mother's furious activity, invasive behavior, and battering, judgmental, critical words. I would often retreat to my room, or if I was in the same room with her I'd stay silent and still to avoid attracting attention. When she did turn her attention to me, she would often start a normal conversation that would unexpectedly turn into an emotionally-charged, unprovoked verbal attack.

Throughout my childhood I was continually on alert, bracing myself for my mother's verbal abuse. This is how I began training as an observer of human behavior, with hands-on experience on how to sense emotions and feel into people's energy fields.

Since I spoke as little as possible, I spent my childhood in my head, reading books and pondering unanswerable questions. Most importantly, I wondered why the people around me were ignoring problems that seemed to be obvious.

I frequently went somewhere in my mind for minutes at a time... to a non-sensory no-place, where I'd be completely blank until my consciousness returned.

Despite being erratic and mentally unstable, my mother was highly intelligent. The morning after she disrupted the family's Thanksgiving dinner by drinking too much and instigating high drama about nothing, I asked her if she wanted to talk about what happened. Looking away from me, she forcefully replied, "Don't get psychological with me."

Over the years, I became very guarded about volunteering any personal information because my mother would pounce on my words, twist their meaning, and later use them in a manipulative way to make me feel badly about myself. If I were happy about anything, she'd be sure to try to find something wrong with it. Because of this, I learned to express no personality and hide any life developments.

Once out of the house, I made dutiful phone calls to her about every other day. When I said hello, she would begin to speak in a stream of consciousness. I continually braced myself for negative comments, which felt as if I was being physically assaulted. I waited for her to finish talking, but then there was more. I just waited until it was over.

Reaching the Breaking Point

As a result of my childhood environment, I had difficulty making choices. I was a good student and a very good, quiet person who followed the rules. I simply allowed others to take charge and make choices for me. At the same time, my mind was continuously churning, trying to figure out why I was in the world, what it all meant, and why any answers that were offered didn't make sense.

After completing my academic studies, I got a job working for the federal government, which was a safe, secure occupation. The woman who hired me had a personality like my mother—she rampaged down office hallways creating drama, and I knew just how to behave in order to get along there.

I met my husband soon after being hired. We were immediately attracted to each other; I was mild-mannered, like his mother, and he had personality traits I instantly recognized.

I had become a captive in a cycle of experiences where I worked for, or had relationships with, people who exhibited my mother's personality traits. I suffered silently, using the same skills I had learned as a child to protect myself from emotional abuse.

As I was being pushed to a breaking point in my seven-year marriage, I consulted a counselor who told me just this: "Do what is best for you." Doing what was best for me offered a new paradigm that I had never considered, and it gave me the courage that I needed. I grabbed on to it for dear life. The day that I left the counselor's office, I took the first step on my journey to wholeness.

My New Path

It became clear that I was responsible for the invisible bonds that held me and I had a lot of personal work to do. Within a year I was divorced, raising four-year-old twins, and working full-time. Because I was navigating my world using childhood survival skills, I was a pleaser who didn't know how to assert myself, express honest thoughts to others, look people in the eye, or relax. But I had a driving desire to improve myself, and so set my foot on the path to a long and winding journey of personal healing.

To start on this journey, I read books by popular spiritual authors, took classes on metaphysical subjects, and networked with like-minded people. It was amazing that it was also the time when the term "self-help" was becoming popular.

I read positive affirmations into a tape recorder and played them over and over while driving to work until I replaced my negative thoughts with positive. I learned holistic healing modalities that enhanced my abilities and shaped my understanding of how we function and relate to others. Most importantly, I made wonderful friends who shared my interests and accepted me for who I was without judgment. We learned together, laughed, cried, hugged, and cared about each other as if we were family.

What I've Learned

I want to thank my mother and the people like her who shaped my experiences, contributing to the insights and abilities I've developed. Without these individuals I would not have been driven to heal myself or acquire the ability to help others.

I developed multi-sensory abilities from an early age, which helped me to read people's energy and identify behavioral traits. I learned that we humans are multidimensional, existing on many levels that most of us don't yet perceive. I've also acquired skills and tools that give me the ability to guide and empower others.

In the same way that I access higher intelligence, I'm able to connect with individuals, in person or by phone, to answer questions and provide them with guidance. If a name is mentioned, I have the ability to provide insight into that individual's energy, emotions, and life circumstances.

Finally, Answers

In September 2013, I created the Formulas4Living.com blog and was very surprised to find that, when I wrote, I was able to put my ego aside and suspend my own thought processes to receive enlightening messages telepathically.

Some people may refer to this as automatic writing or channeling. When I asked questions, I received answers with information that was not within my scope of knowledge or expertise. Also, the vocabulary used in answering my questions was not in my usual manner of speech or writing. At last, I was able to ask about all of the things I wanted to know, receiving amazing, and often mind-boggling, answers.

While adjusting to my new ability, I wanted to identify the source of the messages. At first, I considered that I might be connecting to an Ascended Master or intergalactic group that exists in a higher dimension of the light realms. However, I eventually came to realize that the information I was receiving was not from a source that was outside of myself. Instead, it seemed that I was accessing a higher aspect of my own consciousness that connects with interdimensional wisdom.

This book is an edited compilation of select messages written between September 2013 and April 2016. The questions that I asked are in bold type. The messages offer an enlightened perspective regarding the nature of the human predicament and the value of the Earthly experience. I encourage you to read and absorb the material gradually as a form of meditation, taking time to allow the concepts to permeate your conscious awareness and become a part of your waking reality.

My ability is not unique. In the past few years, there has been an increase in consciousness breakthroughs in which individuals have experienced contact and received transmissions from higher intelligence. Individuals who expand their level of consciousness with the intention of making a connection may interact with star energies that vibrate the highest level of love, peace, and gratitude available.

It is possible for all that exists on Earth to be compatible with this high level of resonance. However, due to the discord of humanity, suffering is a polarizing factor that interferes with maintaining higher states of consciousness. Also, we often sabotage ourselves by inadvertently expressing conflicting, negative resistance to our positive desires.

I consider myself the receiver and transcriber for the messages, which have been written within the constraints of my vocabulary. At times, I didn't fully understand them with my logical mind, but sensed their impact. I believe that the language and concepts expressed are also absorbed by the subconscious. Thus, if you do not immediately grasp the logic or ideas expressed, please be patient and allow yourself to process them on your own level of understanding, knowing that they will be interpreted and comprehended on multiple levels of your Being.

If you find that you resonate with the answers provided, your struggle to understand the puzzle of your identity may be alleviated.

Please remember: There is no judgment and no hierarchy associated with levels of consciousness. We are all in this together. Regardless of any perceptions to the contrary, you are where you need to be in your personal evolution. Each individual is a unique and critical contributor to the evolution of humanity.

We are all in a state of continuous growth and transition. The answers and insights contained in these messages are intended to support and enhance your own process, but not to interfere with it.

Monti Scribner

INTRODUCTION

We all live in varying states of denial; and this is required to maintain our sanity.

We reflect each other and bounce off of each other's energy. We rely on certain functions, abilities, and basic truths as presented and as carried in our DNA. However, this is a fragile system that depends upon a common agreement.

We agree that certain exceptional experiences are facts. We agree that the need to function is a similar experience for everyone. We agree that perfection is achievable if we only try. We agree that there is a common denominator that we strive to meet on a daily basis.

Our story is one of exceptional bravery in the face of uncertainty. We strive for the dream, and react to outside stimuli as if we can control our lives. But that is a lie.

We can only control our character and our responses to outside situations and stimuli.

What we can control, we will. But then we'll ultimately let go of the rest and surrender to uncertainty—to the frightening reality of our existence and to the unknowing. Surrender to the wealth of mysteries that surround us and to the fact that we will never truly know the answers.

But we will keep asking the questions.

CHAPTER ONE:
Not What We Appear to Be

O ur outer appearance and inner nature reflect and assist in forming the experiences we are destined to have. But we are not what we appear to be. When we genuinely express ourselves, we reach for the best possible human experience, whether it's through our conversations, writing, acting, or another form of expression. These instincts to express ourselves reflect our attempts to understand who we are and what our lives are all about.

As mentioned in the preface, these messages will introduce my experience with connecting to a higher level of intelligence, which has offered me the opportunity to ask Universal questions. I realized that when I began to transcribe the answers, I had to put aside my logical mind, because the experience was beyond my ability to comprehend. However, the more questions I asked the more I began to trust and believe the source of the amazing answers.

Changing Paradigms

From a young age, we've been taught to judge everything and everyone we encounter. Conventional society supports our unspoken agreement to participate in the fear-based paradigms, which are composed of limiting belief systems and judgments that profoundly influence our ability to navigate our lives.

The old belief systems prompt us to follow the rules of authoritarian people and institutions. We perceive that we are different from others based upon appearance, causing us to separate from each other.

We now have the ability to relate to our world in a new way by adopting paradigms based on love and by recognizing that we belong to an all-embracing, supportive, cosmic family.

Our Intergalactic Family

What are our origins, and how can we apply that knowledge to benefit us?

It requires a leap of faith to absorb that humans are far more than three-dimensional Beings. Each individual is a multidimensional aspect of a greater Being with their own intergalactic families.

Many individuals are experiencing the next evolutionary step by accessing higher intelligence, which exists outside of the boundaries of the third dimension. By doing so, they receive messages that educate and bring to conscious awareness a higher perspective about their own Being and their participation in the story of humanity.

When individuals open to the frequency that supports

them in receiving telepathic messages from this intelligence, a force field of collective energy is aligned with theirs. This connection will then become instantly accessible so that they may continue to receive answers to questions they ask. Each reply is from the collective unless otherwise stated.

The plan for continued interactions is to assist individuals in experiencing cognitive insights within their capabilities and to create new paradigm channels. Thus, individuals enter into a collective experience in which they participate as members of their intergalactic family.

A Seed of Knowledge

I've always wanted to understand the purpose of our existence on Earth. Can you explain it to me?

You are a product of Universal force expressing nature through a variety of modalities. Your thinking and reasoning ability is a unique function that separates you from the rest of expression on Earth. When you reach for answers to the deeper questions, you make a leap of consciousness to what is available to you right now. This knowledge adheres to your sensibilities and propels you forward into an increased understanding of your place in the Universe.

The carrier* of the genetic makeup for your species allows for an unfolding of consciousness to develop an understanding of your connection to All That Is. However when you seek these answers your comprehension is limited to your language and what you understand in your current reality.

When you ask, "Who is our family?" the connotations are widespread and reach beyond human ancestry to the boundaries of intergalactic parallels. We provide a seed of knowledge to orient your consciousness, and a forward motion is initiated to create an expansion of cognitive ability as allows.

A carrier is a multisensory body that is engineered to facilitate Earth-based experiences.

The Difference Between Us

Why are some of us in physical bodies while others exist in light bodies?

We are here in body just as you are in a body. However, our bodies vibrate at a different frequency so that you can't perceive our ability to exist in a way that is different than yours.

Our intelligence capacity also exists on a scale that is not comparable to yours. Thus we perceive a greater interdimensional picture of how the puzzle pieces fit.

Our perceptions agree with yours in some ways, in that we also believe that the interactions between individuals are a significant factor when participating in the worldview.

What we perceive as the dysfunction of most humans is their inability to grasp the significance of the divinity or sacredness of existence, and then their inability to consciously apply this awareness to daily living. This is the essential difference between us.

When you focus on your 3-D reality, you believe that you exist in a relationship with the earth, sea, and sky, and those aspects of personality representing different relationships.Those relationships are masks or aspects of behavior patterns your Soul needs to interact with in order to learn and grow. All are One in the perfection of Universal experience.

The Human Mask

I've observed that when I go out to shop in my neighborhood, I'm greeted and treated according to the way I appear (of course!). And yet, behind this facade is someone who is very different from my appearance.

So I wonder – what would I look like if my appearance reflected my Soul to others?

What can we do to reconcile the disparity between appearance and Soul essence so that we can be recognized and interact with others more genuinely?

The appearance and nature of an individual does reflect and assist in the experiences they are destined to have; they shape the individual in terms of self-perception and how others interact with them. You are meant to have the human mask that you see in the mirror. But this does not limit you from expressing your true nature, which you do when you articulate your thoughts and feelings.

Hiding Myself

I've often felt that I should limit my self-expression and hide my true self when I interact with people I don't know.

You are a product of a society that squelches individuality. Even those who venture outside the accepted behavior paradigms are accepted for their links to an understandable experience; they are viewed as outliers who are capable of behaving within norms. The issue arises when you do not fit into acceptable standards and express beliefs outside of society's norms.

All established paradigms are based upon the concept of safety and boundaries. In this case you are pushing the boundaries of safety to expose the underlying human fear of not being in control. When you venture outside the boundaries, those individuals who are not prepared or engineered for exploration will become (at a minimum) defensive and judgmental.

Thus, when you express new ideas that the media has schooled the public to view with derision, there is a likelihood of skepticism, and even ridicule.

It is also understandable for you to want to share your new insights and participate in discussions to ground them in your reality. However, this grounding must take place in an environment of acceptance, not derision.

All Beings exist in their own domain of conscious awareness and at different stages of development. The most you can hope for at this time is a forum for discussion while the new paradigms are being introduced since most of these concepts have not reached the hundredth monkey stage of acceptance.

Those who explore these subjects are pioneers, just as you have been a pioneer when you questioned and challenged the boundaries and structure of established thought.

How We Communicate

I sometimes wonder about what reality the people around me are living in compared to the reality that I perceive.

How can we communicate properly in order to truly understand each other?

Your communication in any language characterizes the value of speaking from your heart and stating what you truly mean. Most people couch their language in terms that they believe will be acceptable to their audience; they are not capable of speaking their truth because they have not touched the cord of that aspect of themselves that reflects their deepest nature.

In fact, speaking from the depths of the heart with resonance will only affect the speaker. It will change their ability to relate to and understand themselves because the audience will decipher the communication using their own personal life filters. They filter all that is perceived through their relative experience. Thus, a person speaking from the heart to others will only be heard a percentage of the time and never fully heard.

How then, can we make a real connection with those in our lives who we most care about?

You are a planet unto yourself and yet joined in oneness with All That Is. Your individuation is an illusion and is created from an aspect or fragment of Universal pulse. Ego is the strainer of the filter; thus, without the ego there is no illusion.

Transmutation

I'm so different from the person that I was when I graduated from college. It's as if I've transmuted into another personality with different interests, reactions, perspectives, and desires. If I attended a reunion where people remembered me from that time, it would be like wearing a mask that I couldn't remove.

Do most people transform as they grow older or is my experience unusual?

When an individual arrives on the planet they are already embedded in their life pattern, which nudges them along to have the experiences and interactions meant to provide them with the fertile soil necessary for Soul growth.

You are referring to an aspect of consciousness that embraces the planetary energies and applies to those who are marked for growth in a particular lifetime. When a seed is planted via genetic identification, it is marked for certain experiences such as consciousness expansion, 3-D interactions, and consequences of karmic substance that propels the Soul along its chosen path.

Your lifetime on the planet is a circular experience providing opportunities for Soul growth and interactions that will continue beyond this perceived timeline and have already extended beyond ancestral perimeters.

Enlightenment

What is Enlightenment?

Enlightenment is a term used by humans to define advancement on the spiritual path.

Your Spiritual Library

When I decided to create a blog, I immediately knew that it should be called Formulas4Living. This message, written in November 2013, provided insight into the reason for the domain name:

As you travel along the spiritual path you accumulate a conscious awareness of the concepts you have acquired. These concepts serve as guideposts and can be used to practice personal recognizance.

Your spiritual library includes the knowledge base of concepts gathered but does not always include the formulas for living provided here. These formulas may be added to your knowledge base to offer seeds of information that will upgrade your consciousness to new levels.

The words in these messages are coded to trigger the recognition of spiritual insights. They allow the person reading them to move their awareness down the path towards recognition of insights that may have been previously acknowledged but not necessarily absorbed.

As you read and absorb your consciousness is triggered—a spark ignited. You are aligned with truth as you understand it, and as time goes on you assimilate further. This assimilation matures the brain formation and opens you to even more insights. Allow yourself to simmer with these concepts; absorb them into your thought processes and they will become a part of your virtual reality. In time the terms will be integrated into your vocabulary and more easily accepted as truths.

Who are you to question? You are the only one who is responsible for what you believe and you do not need to accept anything that does not feel right to you. Just be with it, and as time goes on notice what occurs. Your reality will be shifting and adjusting in sync with the concepts you have read.

CHAPTER TWO:
Our Connection to the Universe

I asked many questions related to the complexity of the human experience and multidimensionality. Although the answers I received were objective and sometimes hard for me to understand, I sensed an underlying compassion for the challenges that humans face. I also found it somewhat reassuring that although the Universe functions in an impersonal manner we are being guided as we participate in a Greater Plan.

In these messages you'll see answers about the relationship of difficult life experiences to Soul evolution, the exquisite nature of our existence, the impact of making choices, our connection to a Greater Plan, and our participation in the Universal alignment. The messages will also provide insights into why it's important to stay grounded and maintain a consistent sense of self.

Multidimensionality

I'd like to understand the relationship of 3-D reality to multidimensionality.

In essence, your existence is a mirror of psychological manipulation and an illusion.

Versions of what you would perceive as reality exist on many parallel levels that preclude the intervention of any one Being to alter Divine timing. The correct venue for intervention is in 3-D, where individuals perceive what is real and react only for the purpose of learning their next lesson for Soul growth.

While your reality allows individuals to behave on a level that includes violence, it does not affect the essential compounded nature of the complex relationship between human form and extra-dimensional existence.

The Human Condition

It seems that emotional trauma and suffering are integral elements of the life journey. Is it necessary to suffer in order to evolve?

Know that you are loved and cared for and that the suffering related to the human condition is a construct developed to allow certain experiences to be absorbed and understood. There is no hierarchy as such because all are one in the eyes of the Universe, and the smallest seed has challenges necessary to reach its most advanced state.

If you view the suffering as a personal adventure that develops your character, your insights, and your Soul's ability to mature and not as a personal affront, it will allow you to accept the development of your Soul's path as a magical if challenging source of insights and co-existence with the Universal pulse.

Also, the human condition revolves around Universal truths that extend into the realm of the mysteries. Thus, when a human evolves in consciousness they are circulated in coordination with the biological existence of all manner of life including particles in light realms.

A human on Earth begins their journey for a thousand lifetimes that revolves around lessons to be learned. However, those lessons need not require agonizing experiences regardless of Earth conditions. The agony is often related to choices and decisions having to do with purpose. Thus, those whose purpose is to become an enlightened light being experience conditions that guide them to develop an understanding of Universal principles.

All individuals are engineered to have experiences that will bring them into the realm of enlightenment. However, the definition of enlightenment is a human construct and not completely understood. We see the elevation of consciousness as an opening of DNA that is related to genetic makeup and specific engineering, particularly that of cultural carriers. There are also factors of culture generated within a species that include participating in rites of tribes and not in individual exploration.

Do I understand this to mean that the range of emotions we experience serve an important purpose?

Where a particular experience unfolds in base time, it uncovers the energy of a specific reason for the manifestation of trauma. Thus, a trauma triggers the curve of the arc of emotional experience, logical and illogical reaction, and conclusions reached as a result. This propels you to an understanding not previously integrated into your life experience. You are rebalanced by *every* result associated with a trauma trigger.

While we acknowledge that you do experience multi-layered emotional trauma related to fear, it is an accessory to the process of interaction with a higher level of manipulative Oversoul.* Your Oversoul requires you to experience the range of emotions on this level, which is radiated to all aspects of your being interdimensionally.

Once you free yourself, you will enlighten others. The things that you love and value will not be lost and can remain with you as long as you desire.

An Oversoul is a greater level of consciousness that incorporates and interacts with all levels of your multidimensional Being.

When Navigating Your Reality

Can you give me additional guidance about how to navigate 3-D reality?

Be brave, be patient, and listen to your Soul's longing. Your Soul speaks in human desire, emotions, and symbols. It is forgiving and understanding and it holds your thoughts, prayers, and deepest desires while you navigate your experiences with the tools you have developed over lifetimes.

Knowing that this is not the first, and not the last lifetime, it helps to be aware that belonging to the Universal Soul is a power and a right. To love and be loved is also a right.

To exist is a phenomenon taken for granted, but to be aware that you exist is a relatively new phenomenon created by God Source; and never allowed to be manifested in carriers before now. Your carrier Being is an evolved version of an advanced form.

The genetic makeup of individuals is a template that includes certain dispositions. One of these dispositions is to procreate and to couple. In general, those who couple are included in a security factor that holds them in a degenerative pattern and will not release them to unzip the genetic material included in the new consciousness.

Awareness functions within a purposefully created set of DNA codes to assure arrival at certain conclusions. Where you concern yourselves with inconclusive experiences, you evolve for a kind of manufactured ideal that is not purposefully satisfying. Dissatisfaction is a prompting that generates the idealization of lifetime goals and awareness of loss, which then allows you to dream of greater things.

Your awareness is complexly global and functions interdimensionally as a compass for movement through various delineated counterbalances. Your language evolves within the function of cosmic interference and learned understanding. An allowance for gaps in understanding accepts missteps as inclusive of experience.

Conscious acceptance of new concepts permits coding to be opened.

Picking Your Path

I'm frequently indecisive about the best course of action to take in order to achieve my goals. How can I know if any of the choices I make will be in Divine Order?

When you pick your path and steer your course according to your heart's desire, the choices you make are

Monti Scribner

derived from internal stimulation of energetic threads making soundings or depth charges that manipulate your decisions. Thus, your genetic makeup, your internal coordination, and your personality functions all contribute to steering the course toward your destined path. Your choice is considered to be free will but is actually in alignment with a predestined path taken in accordance with the Greater Plan.

Your participation in the plan is derived by the coordination of interstellar machinations complexly guided by an overarching intelligence—a greater force than human minds can conceive of. Thus, the anguish you may suffer when making choices is actually built into the framework of your genetic makeup and is intended to gather the force of the powerful circuits that coordinate to concern the masses. Either you participate in this dance of life or you are guarded as an outlier until you are forced to transfer the energy into the correct energetic circuit.

Being in the free flow of energy creates no barriers to alignment with the predestined path. If an individual makes a choice that is not in alignment with this free flow, there is a sabotage effect that takes them into negative aspects of experiences and eventually turns them down the compatible path. Alignment of energy can be associated with a manufacturing of goods. Thus, the pieces put together fit as one to create a formula for a successful result. When all pieces fit, the energy is aligned and that portion of the individual's mission is completed.

God's Will

How does God's will participate in this process?

18

We are serving the purpose of Universal alignment which also serves God's will—All Is One.

The Greater Plan

So, we are participants in an objective Greater Plan that is beyond our ability to comprehend or control?

In order for vibratory existence to align with the Greater Plan, an offer of frequency is made to all lines of participation. Thus, all ley lines, all multidimensional frequencies, and all parallel existences are connected via a web of vibratory alignment that occurs in a frequency compatible with the act to be taken. Also, the greater vision of truth allows only that which is in alignment with the frequency to occur.

We understand the overall complexity of this to be too much for individuals wanting to be in alignment and to identify a combination of theories and logical steps to take to manifest and create desired results. However, the connection between a desire and a manifestation is a parallel experience that requires too many interactions outside the realm of understanding to allow one individual to manipulate the outcome. Rather, the release of the desire at the expected frequency and the willingness to participate in subsequent experiences to be guided along the river of life is the safest and most advantageous approach, combining frequency, intention, and understanding. The guiding Universal pulse will allow the individual to experience the highest possible purpose at the moment expected to synchronize with life elements. Be one with the experience and view it with an open heart, open eyes, and loving intention.

The Universal Alignment

How does our level of consciousness affect our participation in the Greater Plan?

As the purpose of all Beings is to be synchronized with the overall plan of existence, each individual is a participant regardless of consciousness. In fact, consciousness plays a part in the process and is integrated into the overall plan. Thus, following your natural instincts and allowing events to unfold once they come to consciousness assures you are fully participating in the Universal alignment. The Universal alignment is a phenomenon of nature that adheres to the Fibonacci* sequence of biological symmetry.

A question arises regarding making conscious choices versus existing in a state of free flow and deliberately avoiding decision-making. In fact, even making the conscious choice to not take action encompasses participation in the overall plan. Thus, your indecisiveness, your emotional traumas, and your choices are all integrated into the Universal alignment for existence on a mass level. If you consider this is the case, then why agonize or exhibit the emotional traumas associated with inability to achieve your heart's desire? This too is an important element in the nature of existence and a manifestation of the human condition.

*The Fibonacci sequence is found in the natural symmetry of nature.

Maintaining Your Sense of Self

How can I be in alignment with my Higher Self while striving for connection with the multidimensional aspects of myself?

All Beings on the planet, regardless of how it appears, are in alignment with a Higher Self, that also connects them to a greater force. This force calibrates them for future experiences and aligns them with the magnetic shifts of the Earth. Thus, your Being is controlled and affected not only by interplanetary forces but by Earth's magnetic forces as well.

The best possible solution for handling this barrage of forces is to stay grounded in your sense of Self. Who you are on a Soul level is accessible to all Beings. Maintaining a sense of Self, regardless of whether completely accurate, may provide balance and clarity in challenging situations.

Those who feel out of sorts may refocus by creating an intention of balance and reconnection with their inner voice. This is critical for interaction with the Higher Self and ultimately the Soul and will not occur unless you maintain a sense of Self.

No individual can truly know themselves, because the conscious search for knowing is within the boundaries of brain formation and inaccessible at this time.

For seekers who maintain a consistent sense of Self, more meaningful interactions with the Soul, the Higher Self, and interplanetary intelligence will become available.

Frequency

What is frequency?

Frequency is the vibratory integer that aligns each individual with a specific path. When you adjust your frequency to the intentions you hold you are aligned with a certain configuration of energy that supports you on your path and the bumpy road becomes smoother.

Vibration

What is vibration?

In this context, vibration is the adjusted frequency of each entity that exists in multi-levels on and off the planet. Its vibratory rate is aligned with its Soul's purpose and includes a factor of personality system and internal understanding, which is connected to the Higher Self and Oversoul.

What we want to explain is that the vibration of carrier frequencies alerts the Being to direction. Thus, tuning in to the sense of current or energy associated with personal alignment preserves the correct service of the Universal pulse.

Participation in the unity of oneness assures that each individual is a facet of wholeness regardless of conscious choice. Accepting this as fact assures the typical individual will be in synchronicity with a given plan.

When abundant energy is exerted to persist in a direction not in keeping with Universal pulse, this resistance affects the polarities of the Earth plane, diverging the planetary alignment into chaotic overflow. Thus, the dangerous situation is created where the edge of catastrophe is teetering on the rim of darkness. We say to you, participate in the alignment of oneness as a barrier to frequency overload and ballast to negativity.

CHAPTER THREE:

What Is Real? Recognizing Guidance

It took some time for me to understand and accept that my perceptions were illusions. I asked many questions about the 3-D experience and our place in the Grand Plan (Who Am I?), along with a series of questions about how to recognize, receive, and validate guidance from higher intelligence. I wanted to get as much information as possible about how to recognize authentic connections.

If Life Is an Illusion, What Is Real?

How can I tell the difference between what is an illusion and what is real?

Your choice of wording for this question (if life is an illusion, what is real?) excludes a multitude of possibilities regarding your perceptions. You are actually perceiving, sensing, and experiencing things while evolving through a preconditioned environment. If you walk through a wall is it real? If you perceive a situation a particular way is it also real?

Your version of reality allows for the creation of an environment that supports your Soul growth, and the experiences you have created are triggering various physiological functions supporting that growth.

Focus on staying in balance regardless of how you perceive these experiences. This will allow you to continue to evolve while recognizing the function of spirit and of perceived situations as guideposts to personal growth.

Understanding your experiences is not necessary. But how you react to them affects their value as guideposts.

Who Am I?

Please help me to understand who I am in relation to the Greater Plan.

You are a member of a species that is characterized by a vision of the Universe for a long-range illumination of time. There are no boundaries to the Universal force and you exist on a plane of conversion from animal to conceptual human. The human was created as a sub-set of carrier to connect with a version of species that will walk the earth in thousands of years. This is a flash of time not conceptualized by your mind, but in the grand scheme of things it will not matter.

The long-range plan is to design a new subspecies that is elegant in its form and abilities. Peace will reign on this planet and outlanders, or mutants that are not in alliance with new forms will be eliminated.

An oversight of planetary realignment exists that views the current situation of barbaric behavior beyond toleration and it will be stopped. A coercion plan exists with a timeline for generations to be re-formed as unable to create violence. A more harmonious existence is being modeled and aligned with current perspective but will be hundreds of years in the making.

A new brain formation is also necessary with a viewpoint to cloud the vision of those unable to accept new paradigms. The old-school thinkers will be relegated to a short lifetime in order to allow upgraded Beings to inhabit the planet as envisioned.

Again, this realignment will be an anatomically-correct human form, with new perspectives and vision for future improvements. Interdimensional Beings are engineering a subspecies to be introduced in this century that will plant the seed for realignment.

Current brain formations are balanced toward numbness, or toleration, of a certain level of deaths in favor of what is determined to be freedom. This mindset and certain other old school mindsets are version 1.0 of genetic creation, but must die out with this generational shift. Then, new thinking and a new approach will gradually come to pass. This will not happen until a destructive level of behavior becomes so intolerant that it can no longer be ignored.

You Are Limitless

How does my individual experience make a difference?

Who you are on Earth and why you exist requires an understanding of cosmology.* However, the greater your leap in consciousness, the greater the understanding and knowing of the truth of your existence.

You exist continually on a plane of existence that can be called a constellation for expansion.

Your personal expansion is occurring on a continual basis and intergalactic connections arise as a result of your heritage originating in the stars. A perfect example of this is the carrier of truth, Mahatma Gandhi. This ascended master walked the earth to demonstrate connection and expansion of fairness to all. His peaceful manner demonstrated and emanated an understanding of equality, and his affirmation of peace continues to circulate on etheric levels.

We ask you to consider that all who existed in the past and those to come, as well as those living on the planet now, form a consortium of levels of interaction that fulfills the term of cosmology.

Thus, the inclusion of a new level of consciousness embraces all current, past, and future circumstances and allows the opening for expansion to perpetuate the Universal core. You are in an eternal cycle of acquiring wisdom and expanding limitlessly.

Cosmology is the study of the origin and development of the Universe.

Receiving Guidance from Higher Intelligence

How can I identify when I'm receiving guidance from higher intelligence, and how can I be sure that the messages I'm receiving are accurate and valid?

Manage your existence on a higher level by noticing your thoughts and external interactions. Guidance can exist between your thoughts. Verbal interaction is only a small part of what you receive and process.

To validate that the information you receive is based in truth, sense the feeling associated with it. Your body is a tuning fork that resonates in balance with Universal truths. An open, spacious feeling indicates acceptance and validation of what is offered.

Please explain telepathic holography. Is this a common form of communication between higher intelligence and humans?

Telepathic holography is a process used to transfer thoughts in order to convey the whole of an idea or vision to another. The transmitter's vision must be sharp, and intent clear, to complete this transference accurately. More advanced Beings are able to transmit a holography of thought with image to receptive individuals who are ready for this experience.

In fact, different levels of these messages are frequently transmitted and the receiver often assumes that they are self-delivered or original ideas. Ideas associated with technological advancements and inventions have been received in this way.

This evolution of a paradigm is being introduced via multiple modalities to open conscious awareness to a life-enhancing partnership with higher intelligences.

How do I know whether an idea is my own or a transmission received via telepathic holography?

Your purpose must be clear before beginning the process with the intent of receiving and verifying communication. Start by noticing visions and concepts that surpass your current library of knowledge and experience. The purpose is to expand your sensitivity and open your insights to new paradigms and new ways of living beyond the five senses.

Is this the next frontier for conscious individuals?

Many individuals already receive holographic images accompanied by thought. They identify them as their own. This next step is to consider that some of your visions and thoughts are transmitted, or planted, via telepathy from more advanced intelligence. We caution you to be discerning and not to accept a transmission that conflicts with your sense of morals, stability, and individuality. If the experience shifts your awareness to a new thought level and creates a positive reaction within your sense of Self, continue to explore and process what you've received.

How can I improve my ability to receive these transmissions?

We ask that you suspend judgment and animation when we speak to you to allow us to fully permeate your consciousness. We speak in tongues, symbols, sounds, and words. But our strength lies in the accomplishment of energetic transmission of pictures. The pictures convey an interdimensional aspect of creation not understood through other forms of communication.

The spoken and written word only allows what we can translate through our language to yours. Any language contains limited availability of concepts and words necessary to explain what we have to convey.

The picture for you today is a swan swimming across a still pond. There are few ripples on the pond created by the swan gliding atop the water. Notice that the swan does not exhibit excess movement; its wings are folded and its head is bent as it glides along the water.

This picture demonstrates that when you center your awareness in the present and continue on your path without effort you will more easily navigate the waters of your life.

Experience the inner calm and stillness of the swan. It knows that it will reach its destination, without urgency. This inner knowing is deeply held in consciousness. Imagine being a part of All That Is and emulate the experience of the swan.

Some people say that they receive messages that are identified as being from a collective and others from an individual entity. For example, my friend said she received messages from the Masters as a collective, and many people get messages from individual energies like Jesus.

The personas that provide you with messages and insights come from a variety of locations in the Pleiades, astral associative collectives, auric fields, and more. In fact, these personas are a conglomeration of intelligences that identify themselves in ways that you will be able to understand.

Also, the tenor of the messages can be attributed to different personality archetypes such as angelic, authoritative, and guiding. These sources flavor their messages with information and guidance compatible with the expectation of the receiver. They also provide information that will be understood at the receiver's level of consciousness.

For this reason, certain directives are associated with different personas and received from various collectives. However, the coordination of who will provide and receive this information is orchestrated in a way to heal, guide, and provide a cooperative message that will be received appropriately. There is no difference between a single sender and a collective except that they are calibrated to communicate with the receiving individual.

Please explain why I occasionally receive messages from the Hathors rather than from other intelligences.

Your messages are from the Hathors because you are calibrated vibrationally to associate with this dimensional intelligence. Your heritage provides a connection with the Hathors. There is also a version of communication that is generic and can be received by all who are open to this form of transference. The complex nature of transference depends upon the level of the receiver and the intentional calibration of the sender to the receiver's vibration.

The People in Your Life

I've noticed that many of the people who were in my circle of friends a few years ago are no longer in my life, and yet I've continued friendships with several wonderful women who I met over 20 years ago.

For perspective on your path, notice the people who are currently in your life and think about whether these same people were in your life a year ago. Identify who is relatively new and who is no longer in your immediate circle. Then, consider viewing the newer people as an indication of the Divine coordination of your personal constellation.

Although achieving your Soul purpose does not depend upon maintaining mature relationships; if certain relationships are not in alignment with your path they will fall away.

As mentioned before, there can be no judgment about where you are on your path or what you have achieved. The primary purpose of your Soul's guidance is to provide a map to the recognition of your divinity and unity with All That Is.

So, the more you maintain conscious awareness that you are one with all things, the more you will be in sync with your Divine Plan.

Life as a Story

At any given time, there have been multiple major and minor characters that have participated in my story. Even a simple conversation with a stranger that seemed to be insignificant at the time has served to provide support for making a big life decision. For example, a t-shirt vendor that I met in the Charleston Market told me his tale of how he came to live in Charleston, which positively contributed to my eventual decision to move there.

If the people in your life serve as mirrors, helping you to understand yourself, then when you disconnect or cease a relationship it can indicate that the lesson or experience you were meant to have is completed.

When this happens to you, do you thank them and move on, or do they continue to be on the periphery of your life?

Your daily experiences encompass an ebb and flow of gradual consciousness changes that create a new life in every moment. When you wake up in the morning, are you the same person who went to sleep last night? On a superficial level, you operate as if you are the same. But in multiple and important ways, you are different.

What were you thinking about before you went to sleep last night? Did that subject stay with you this morning, and how do you feel about it now?

You tend to be aware of the continuity of subject matter but rarely track the path an idea takes to its conclusion. If you did, your mind would be full of minutia and unable to handle all incoming experiential traffic. Thus, the ebb and flow of change carries with it an understanding of who you are so you have an identity touchstone, and the change that occurs is a volume that would represent a continuing T.V. miniseries.

If you think about your life as a story and identify the key characters, which are primary characters, secondary characters, and so on? This analysis is important in enabling your consciousness to transcribe your development and help you with direction when necessary.

You enjoy the ebb and flow when it comforts and supports you. You may resist it when it shakes your world, shocks your system, and eventually moves you to a different state of awareness.

There is also an aha moment associated with each transformative experience when you process and allow it to speak to you.

Recognizing and accepting the value of your ebb and flow experiences is a gift that you give to yourself.

CHAPTER FOUR:
Manifesting in 3-D Reality

A mong all the questions and answers that I posted on my Formulas4Living website, I received the most interest from my readers about manifesting what we want. Questions such as, "Why are we so determined to have a backup plan?" were a running theme. In the following messages, you'll see the various ways I approached this subject to obtain the most helpful answers.

Manifestation and Emotion

So many people give advice about how to manifest what you want. When I try to apply what I've learned, it seldom produces the desired results.

Holding the vision of alignment with a Divine Master Plan strengthens the attraction to positive manifestation.

A mistaken perception of how to create or manifest what you desire requires you to think hard about what you want while focusing only on the positive emotion associated with it. We say, allow the true emotion to precede the wish for new creation.

Without allowing yourself to feel the lack of what you desire, you suppress true emotion in the field of the body, which stops the function of natural creation. A suppressed feeling of sadness, overridden by false hope and forced positivity, creates a muddle of disjointed messages sent out to the Universe. These conflicting messages cross and neutralize each other.

Further, the body holding conflicted feelings becomes congested with blocked energy, which contributes to physical problems.

The technique that instructs to love and accept yourself for what you are feeling, such as the Emotional Freedom Technique, facilitates a positive approach to identifying suppressed emotion and may support the initial process for eliminating bad feelings that interfere with balanced function.

Welcome the availability of a full range of emotions to guide you along your path. Intuitive healers and body workers value the enriching influence of emotions when connecting with their clients. Although it is possible that excessive feeling may influence a person unnecessarily, you can also be served by sensing the range of emotions transmitted by your body in order to process your reactions to certain experiences.

Dissatisfaction contains a level of emotion that triggers a complex array of indications that a course can be altered to improve your level of enjoyment. We encourage you to take the temperature of your feelings frequently, allowing them to guide you.

How accurate are emotions in guiding us when making decisions?

Your decisions are made on many levels with many considerations, but emotions should certainly play a part in your decision-making process. How you feel when you consider a course of action is an internal guidance system that allows you to be comfortable when a choice is being made.

When to Wait, When to Act, How to Know

How do we know when to wait for something to manifest versus when to act or when to chart a different course?

Your question is based in logic, arising from your own ability to reason. However, there is no reason associated with this issue. The person who lives in a world created by mass consciousness is not alone in their quest to arrive at a destination that is in synchronicity with their desires. However, there are many, many virtual and interdimensional cords associated with each action taken on the planet. It is beyond your capability to comprehend or master these issues. Our advice is as follows:

- Take the situation as it occurs in your present time and consider it from all angles.
- Sit in it until you have a quiet understanding of how you feel about it. Consider all emotional attachments, desires, and contributions from others who have no investment in the outcome.
- Then, turn it around in your mind. Consider it objectively, viewing it from the outside as if it is not you who is experiencing it.
- From this perspective, release all inhibitions and

preconceived ideas regarding the issue or situation.

- Then you may gain a knowing or understanding of the situation that will allow you to move away from it or become unstuck. Only when you release all attachments and are ready to shift from personal to impersonal will you shift in your perspective.

Your preconceived ideas about how something should be or the results you would like to achieve will inhibit the necessary shift into a new paradigm of understanding.

Free Will

What is the role of free will in the manifestation process? That's what comes to mind when the virtual interdimensional cords, actions, and mass consciousness are mentioned.

When you consider free will, or the definition of free will, as you understand it, you believe that you have the ability to create an outcome and that you have the ability to make choices that will lead to an expected outcome. In many cases, a desired outcome can be achieved.

However, there is also a chaotic avenue that may propel you onto another path. This is reliant on the subtleties of combined creation. In combined creation there is an individual and then there are many factors previously described, including those who will be impacted by the individual's choices.

Free will is optimal when you put your ego aside to align yourself with your Soul purpose. To do so it is necessary to create a vision of the optimal outcome, put it aside, and then allow yourself to set out in favor of combined chaos. The chaos that commences is a result of decisions made and the puzzle pieces will eventually align, but not without the chaos occurring. This creates a spinning effect that channels creation.

When you conceive of creation you believe that it will result in an outcome of fairness as you understand it, but that is your personal viewpoint. Fairness is not a factor. Universal alignment creates the outcome, not the person exercising free will.

So, is it within our capability to manifest what we want?

The purpose of the human experience is not to learn the process of manifestation but to exercise free will to the extent possible and to learn the lessons associated with decisions made. The manifestation that results from this is an outlying effect of desire.

There are certain basic desires included in the DNA package intended to maintain the procreation and continued existence of the species. Beyond following these basic desires, individuals pursue their own predestined path to learn conscious awareness, which is a building block of conscience, and to experience interactions influenced by planetary shifts. Thus, the question, "Can we manifest what we want?" is not answered with "yes" or "no."

However, the choices that you make influence probabilities. When a desire is within the Soul's path and also in alignment with all aspects of your path, you may achieve your desire. There can be as many unseen contributing factors for the birth or manifestation of a desire as there are biological factors that contribute to the creation and birth of a baby.

Please explain more about why we may not be able to manifest what we want despite our best efforts.

The true picture is a panorama beyond the imagination or ability for you to see.

What you want is conditioned by mass consciousness and the underpinnings of the society where you reside. As mentioned before, you are biological Beings that are a part of nature with a predetermined structure and path in alliance with your Soul's purpose. And, many desires are the result of DNA-influenced categories of life-sustaining factors.

To question an experience is a given. You are meant to react to and challenge those things that you question. Your exertion of free will is also built into your genetic makeup. When something does not happen the way you would like or expect it to, this triggers the will and the awareness needed to examine and rethink your path. It is all in alignment with a predestined path.

The stretching and exercises necessary to grow your consciousness are available to you. However, the information immediately available to you is limited. The gradual unfolding of new consciousness is a process that cannot be rushed any faster than the pace of nature to evolve a new microcosm of life. This new consciousness has been planted and the seed is germinating.

Understanding Experiences

In a previous response, you stated, "Understanding your experiences is not necessary. But how you react to them affects their value as guideposts." Why isn't it necessary to understand my experiences?

Your experiences rotate depending on the lifetime you choose to focus on. Each contains a story with a germ of potential for Soul growth.

Rather than focusing on the meaning of the experience, describe how it makes you feel and be conscious of the next steps that you take as a result of having the experience. The experience itself is a stepping-stone to a new realization for Soul growth, but in itself it is meaningless.

When you follow the insights derived from this level of experience they will lead you to new understanding about who you are and what you believe.

Instead of asking, "What did this experience mean?" or "Why did it happen?" ask, "What did I learn as a result of this experience?" In this way, you become aware of the wisdom you acquired as a result of the experience.

The Pursuit of Perfection

I sometimes think that if I can do everything correctly I won't have bad experiences.

You are allowed to be imperfect. The pursuit of perfection is highly overrated; perfection is solely in the eye of the beholder.

Allow yourself to relax into your Being. Generate feelings of relaxation throughout your body and realize that ideas, concepts, new energy, and impulses flow more easily from this perspective.

As you relax, reflect on the humor associated with the human condition. How silly of us to believe we are at the center of the Universe and that what we perceive is all that there is.

Be aware that your existence is a speck in the eye of the Universe and yet essential to the function of the Universal alignment.

Laugh today.

Impatience

Why is impatience a part of the human makeup?

When you are impatient you assume that time exists and is a factor in carrying out the fulfillment of your desires.

You have recognized that impatience is not one pure emotion but is a combination of emotions that indicate unhappiness with a situation. And, you recognize that it is an indicator of a personal issue that can be resolved with further examination.

When you sense that you are impatient about a situation, you are expressing unhappiness with yourself or your current status with respect to your life. However, there are deeper issues that should be addressed for complete resolution. Be aware that there are no boundaries to the eventual expansion of understanding once you take this as an opportunity to explore.

Impatience speaks to an unwillingness to allow events to unfold as they should and evolve on their own, trusting that all will fall into place. Impatience also speaks to your availability for events to happen and to your inability to reconcile with the orderliness of a Greater Plan.

Thus, you may have forgotten that nature's pace is also your pace. Instead you are sensing urgency. In many cases

NOT WHAT WE APPEAR TO BE

you do not want to wait for things to develop or open as they follow a path to fruition.

When you are impatient, you are listening to that part of your ego that wants more, that wants developmental acceleration, and that also participates in anxiety-causing activities.

What is our best course of action when we feel impatient?

It may help to follow the impatient feeling into your past and identify a time when you felt the same way. In the majority of cases, you felt this way when you were a baby wanting to be fed. As you waited for your parent to feed you, your bodily functions began to feel urgency as if you would never receive sustenance. And so, impatience is a cry for sustenance and completion—for the ability to complete all actions as you would like them to be.

When you feel impatient, think about this: you will be fed, you will receive, and all will be given in the pace of natural order.

Please clarify the statement that "all will be given."

In the natural order, all is given and completed. However, the version of completion that the ego or conscious awareness prefers is not necessarily the version that is on the agenda for the individual's experience.

Is there anything else you can tell me about impatience?

When you recognize that you are impatient, there is opportunity for you to explore your current situation and understand aspects of your ego that wants more than you have. The Soul is also participating in this experience, triggering the ego to create the thoughts and feelings necessary to move you along your path. Introspection about why you are feeling impatient can result in significant personal insight.

Achieving Goals

What else can you tell me about how to achieve goals?

When you are unfocused or your focus is split between different options your ability to manifest a particular goal is virtually at an impasse. We react in dismay when we view the human tendency to scatter energy among many different options in order to achieve a goal.

Identify the goal and then set the boundaries and intentions for manifestation. Your purity of spirit and intention, as well as the obvious regard for other individuals involved in achieving the goal, are important factors in final achievement.

How does this relate to the tendency to be impatient?

In many cases impatience is a result of the inability to achieve your desires. However, it is also a symptom of lack of focus regarding exactly what you wish to manifest. Think about what is making you impatient and identify the systemic course of the frustration that has lead to it.

Where there is a desire that is not fulfilled, there is a course of action that has been taken and dead-ended or blocked. If you have not at least taken steps toward your goal, then you have no reason to be impatient.

Focus on your desire and why you want to achieve it. Identify why you have developed the need for this and why you are impatient. Then, identify the qualities that you possess that will contribute to the achievement of your desires. If you cannot do these things you will continue to wander in a maze of unfulfilled desires.

There is another aspect to this process—once you have put the effort into examining the motives behind your desires you may find that a particular goal does not shine so brightly, but it will lead you down a brighter path.

Please elaborate on the idea that a course of action has been blocked or dead-ended. Why would this be the case?

This message assumes that you have taken a course of action toward your desired goal and you are disappointed that you have not been able to manifest your desire. In this case we suggest that you examine your motives for wanting to achieve that particular goal and reassess the situation. What do you perceive is standing in the way of achieving your goal? What is happening in your life that you might not be noticing? And what is your heart telling you in regard to the goal you believe you wish to reach?

Emotions play an important part in this type of situation where you may be so focused on achieving your goal that you are not in touch with the sensory aspects of the experience. We suggest that you stop, reconnect with your senses, and then ask yourself what you are feeling about the situation and what message your emotions may be giving you. This also requires that you be truthful with yourself. With some introspection you may decide that a different path is in order.

Having a Backup Plan

Why are we so determined to have a backup plan?

The question that we would ask is," Do you believe that you will be given a parachute so that you may have a soft landing in the field of life?" Most people do not trust that they will be given a parachute or that they will land in a soft field versus a hedge filled with thorns. For that reason, many people who set goals or take action toward their goals create a backup plan for the eventualities that might occur.

However, the ego creates a minefield of opportunities for the imagination to run wild, creating so many possibilities that people often lose sight of their original goal. So, people always identify their goals, but it can be healthy to identify one or two other avenues in the event that their goals are not manifested as desired.

What is the nature of humanity? That you imagine you are walking down a perfect path in a perfect life that will end at a calm harbor with a yacht waiting, in which you will sail off into calm waters. What a boring life that would be. Instead, those with adventurous hearts and caring natures stop along the way to help others, take detours, and embrace the change that occurs with every turn of the path. Yes, there will be brambles and thorns, but there will be consciousness-raising experiences to delight and surprise. We welcome and embrace the surprises and unexpected turns in the path and we hope that you will, too.

Divine Timing

How can we know when we are in the flow of Divine Timing rather than forcing an experience?

When you live in your heart and see through eyes of appreciation and love, you view all experiences as being in Divine Order. However, when you resist the flow and attempt to manipulate the outcome of events, you may perceive that resistance. If so, stop and re-examine your motives and the motives of the other individuals participating in the drama.

Meeting Basic Needs Versus Following Soul Guidance

When I notice that I'm worrying about finances, I frequently affirm that I always have more money than I ever need. When I pay a bill, I do it with a feeling of gratitude that I have sufficient funds.

How do we reconcile the basic need to support ourselves with the messages from spirit to follow Soul guidance?

There does not need to be a conflict between Soul guidance, spiritual pursuits, and activities required to support your lifestyle. When you keep an eye on the clock and your heart is invested in a money-generating activity, the result is a loss of life energy and declining spark.

Consciously cultivate your identity as a powerful and empowered Being. Otherwise, the powerlessness associated with earning an income in a way that conflicts with your life force will degenerate the body and Soul, resulting in a shorter life span.

When you allow material things and finances to dictate your direction you avoid the eyes of the Soul and the direction of the heart. Be conscious of and choose those things that support your growth.

Live with a goal of supporting your spirit with life-enhancing activities and allow the nature of source to support you.

Geographic Location

I woke up one morning with a clear thought of needing to visit Glastonbury, England. I didn't know anything about Glastonbury but had a strong feeling urging me to go there. So I made travel plans with an itinerary including time in London, a visit to Stonehenge, and a few days in Glastonbury. I enjoyed the entire experience but never received any insights about why I was guided to go there.

Is our geographic location significant to our development and if so, for what reasons?

Your development and Soul growth is influenced by many factors, and one of them is geographic location. When you are situated in a certain place on the planet, the vibrations from Earth's crust, the planetary influences, and ley lines all contribute to trigger the ability to arrive at solutions, evaluate your decisions, and to take actions in certain directions.

Your location influences thought processes as well as relationships because you will relate to others drawn to that location. The connections and bonds made in particular locations will continue to influence you regardless of how long you remain there. Thus, a short trip to a new city will trigger certain synapses, thought processes, and energetic occurrences, which can help or hinder a body and Soul.

A Foot on the Path

Is it best to just allow the Universe to unfold our experience?

A foot on the path towards your goal allows you to

find the clues that will lead you to your desired destination. However, without placing your foot on the path with awareness and intent you will eventually arrive at the same destination.

The choice is yours; in the grand scheme there is no difference between taking action with intent and allowing the Universe to unfold your experience without effort.

It would be nice if I could be sure that I'm making the right choice so I won't have to retrace my steps or start again.

There is no right or wrong. However, ignoring an inner prompting is also a choice that can lead to further Universal prompting. The inner prompting is the voice of the Universe allowing you to evolve at your own pace but also at the desired stage of your development.

Also, when you consciously choose from an array of options in the spectrum of your life, you automatically experience the vibratory repercussions of that choice throughout time and space. It feeds your consciousness, winds around your vibratory field, and carries the essence of your intention into the experience as if it has been completed.

Even flipping through the pages of a magazine and resonating with a photo creates a spark of recognition that affects your holographic experience.

Thus, all choices and experiences contribute to the Whole, even down to the smallest interaction that does not register consciously. Your Being is continually absorbing and reacting on an elemental, or vibratory level.

Meditation can be used to connect and integrate these experiences by balancing the outward with the inward, bringing the vibratory frequency to a lower level, contributing to the cyclic union of all aspects of your Being to the Whole.

You are being given the support and nurturance necessary to achieve your desired state in this lifetime. Listen to your inner voice; notice how these thoughts make you feel. Consider taking action. Place your foot on the path according to these promptings.

CHAPTER FIVE:
Polarities and the Drama Game

In the following exchanges, I delve deeper into the subject of the drama games we tend to play while walking on this Earth. When asking whether love is really the glue that binds the Universe, I received a very interesting response, as well as an unexpected answer for why bad behavior is repeated.

On a personal level, I wanted to know how a lack of parental love affects our path and to learn more about the effects of dysfunctional family dynamics. The answers I received traced back into history—all the way back to the destruction of Atlantis.

The Drama Game

How do we stop playing the drama game?

The drama game is the basis for experiencing polarities on the planet. Nothing allows you to opt out of experiencing polarities. However, you can choose to become an objective observer and analyzer, precluding emotional participation.

How do we avoid being emotionally triggered in polarizing situations?

There is no rule about this issue. A person with an investment in the outcome of a particular issue will be challenged. To avoid being triggered requires conscious self-discipline and a high level of awareness.

Where there is an investment in the outcome of a situation, Divine Timing can be skewed. But when an individual allows a situation to unfold and steps into the process as a neutral but interactive participant, Divine Timing is activated.

In a sense, all of nature participates in Divine Timing, and as biological Beings humans participate in their own way. However, conscious awareness and choices made will affect the scope and timing of a situation.

When an individual adds negative emotional energy to a drama, it exerts a force that can be termed "nomad" that rotates and warps it. Then, the drama will travel a different, undefined route to the outcome.

To keep on course to a result that will be in Divine Order, focus your awareness on allowing a situation to unfold without negative interference.

Love and the Human Heart

How is it that the emotion of love is the glue that binds the Universe? Is this so?

Yes, when you reverse the magnetics of Universal flow it results in the association of emotional context to the human heart. The beating heart reflects the pulse of expansion throughout the magnetic fields and the connection of all in this construct to the Greater Plan.

Please explain, "When you reverse the magnetics of Universal flow, it results in the association of emotional context to the human heart."

The electrical resonance of nature, which includes emotional context, affects the Universal pulse. This mechanism connects human existence to the relationship between all molecular forms. The heart participates in this greater scheme. Its beats, electrical charges, and emotional interactions also affect the operation of the Universal pulse.

Rewards for Bad Behavior

Why do some people repeat bad behavior even though they should know better?

Fabrication of emotions or manipulation of qualities attempting to manifest a particular result are inexperienced attempts to understand and master the third dimension. This dimension responds to the polarities of peaceful coexistence and violent expression. However, the inexact creation of human biology and the attempt to manipulate self-expression have resulted in counterintuitive behavior being rewarded. Thus, rewards for bad behavior. Even when an individual expresses bad behavior, the reaction of society reinforces their actions. Most individuals feed on the attention they receive regardless of how punitive it may be.

Family Dynamics

How do family dysfunctions affect our ability to evolve?

Your family dynamics reflect the paradigm that you are meant to heal in this lifetime. Thus, when your parents are incapable of loving you for whatever reason, your faith in yourself is tested and your ability to master the confusion resulting from lack of love and reaching for unrealized affection creates a broken energy field that relates to carrying a burden of cellular incompletion. Because your cellular makeup is nurtured by the continuous ebb and flow of the Universe, all cells work to maintain the balance associated with participation in that dynamic.

How do we heal a broken energy field?

Paradigms relate to expression of Self in an infinite cycle of lifetime experiences. A broken energy field is a participant in the cycle of life and is usually related to a small incident that occurs in the interaction between the Soul and the Universal force. It is projected into your life experience, creating an impression that expands its importance and triggers emotional reactions outside the scope of conscious understanding. Thus, the comprehension of a trauma echoes throughout a lifetime, creating ripples as when a stone is tossed into a pond.

Healing a broken energy field relaxes the association between trauma and perceived injury. A conscious understanding of the source of the trauma and the perception of injury is the first step in releasing it from your cellular memory as an incomplete or fractured view of reality.

When you consciously connect with your energy field and carry it forward, you will gain insight into decisions that are associated with these traumas. For example, why would you yearn for a love relationship rather than focusing on your relationship with yourself? You may realize that an incomplete self-image created the paradigm for interaction that was adjusted to reflect your self-view. Your view, or conscious creation of life experience, would then be a direct result of your image of yourself as it relates to your family programming.

When you accept the circumstances of your family origins as the seed for your future Self and rid yourself of assumptions having to do with motivations, you release the concept of victimhood and correlate the current reality you have created to a new vision: one that you can create in a positive manner.

Healing a broken energy field creates the circumstances for the positive seeding of a new experience more in keeping with your vision of achieving the completion of a negative cycle.

Shaped by Experience

I don't know what it's like to experience unconditional parental love. Does it make a difference in human development to grow up knowing you are cared for and unconditionally loved?

The event you are looking for is one of the seed being nurtured to blossom like a tree with all its lovely green foliage, reaching its roots into healthy soil and being fed what it needs to grow. In this case, the caring and love become the fertile soil for you to develop healthy patterns and lives. However, even if there is love, it does not mean there will not be other traumatizing experiences to cause an individual to mutate, encountering psychological hurdles that affect the ability to develop a healthy adult life.

In fact, there are so many barriers and considerations connected to developing an individual that there is no sense in trying to understand the part that human interactions play. You are in a spiral of learning that has to do with karmic patterns and cycles; this spiral of learning creates an environment that makes individuals aberrate. The aberration is the unique quality that differentiates each person. Like snowflakes, no two are alike.

The qualities that contribute to each individual include a mix of genetic heritage, DNA, and star seed. Those who are not generic are individuated by character and pattern type. So, the engineering is a result of altering DNA and contributing elements of star seed patterns in certain varieties of humans.

It is not the love or lack of love—it is the reaching for a certain balance, understanding, and equilibrium that creates a drive or motivation to achieve the experience of being fully individuated. Thus, the messages encoded in DNA include a characterization of individuality and a purpose-driven need for self-expression. All disappointments are treasured as guideposts to life targets. There are no mistakes.

Partners

It seems unfair for people who long for a partner, sometimes for an entire lifetime, to be denied that experience. Why do some people have partners and others do not?

Your visual reality includes a particular recognition of double inclusion, which is a partner who reminds you of a piece of yourself that you lack. You will be attracted to that piece of the atomic solution that joins you in an eternity of connection as if your puzzle pieces are connecting magnetically. However, this connection is with your Self.

When you recognize that the partner you include in your life is an aspect of your Being, you will become conscious that the interactions between you two are formulas for solutions. Your solutions include bearing the reminder that there is an Eternal Being connected to you—your Soul—and that your connective concepts include those who reflect your solutions to ultimately merging with All That Is.

Those who may misinterpret the reason for their lack of a partner are asked to recognize that the internal partnership continues, and the journey includes all aspects of interactions, both loving and not, intended to bring them to the State of Oneness.

The longing for a partner is a biological function that encourages procreation but also resolution of internal conflicts created by dysfunction. Thus, continual interaction with partners produces a conductive resonance that emanates beyond the auric field and results in imperceptible solutions.

Being in a mindset of gratitude regardless of whether you have a partner may result in the State of Bliss, which meets at the crossroads of all resolved interactions.

Extreme Polarities

What Beings and energies are connected with Atlantis?

The story of Atlantis is an example of how a combination of extreme polarities can reach a destructive tipping point.

Many individuals on the planet have experienced, and some may recall, lifetimes in Atlantis. The connection with Atlantis involves technological experiments that went awry. What was originally created as an ideal civilization crystallized into an evolutionary disaster that was triggered by advanced, highly evolved Beings who possessed significant blindness to their own flaws.

We view this experience as one of failure with one exception. We took the kernel of experience and knowledge from that civilization to create truths that can be applied to the current architects of this civilization.

Despite the drawbacks associated with humanity that exists on Earth at this time, there is no fatal flaw that will completely destroy all on the planet. We view nuclear energy as controllable, and the intelligence of those who believe they can control it to the detriment of others is deficient enough to characterize them as lower level: incapable of wreaking complete destruction, although they would like to think otherwise.

Now, the egoic nature of Atlanteans spurred them to reach beyond their capabilities. That, combined with their advanced abilities, tipped the balance of life into destructive conditions that could not be salvaged.

Those people living on the planet now who have a memory, or sense, of Atlantean energy or dream of drowning, are crystallized in a condition of failure. They carry the failure of that civilization along with the dream of an ideal existence, which results in their inability to take action. Thus, when these individuals, although brilliant, conceive of a highly evolved solution to a problem, their memory of failure results in an inability to complete their concept or develop it to fruition.

Our view of these individuals is that they must complete their actions or be destined to repeat these patterns in future lifetimes. The cycle of frustration requires a break in egoic focus, which is a humbling experience for Beings who conceive of themselves as perfect.

The solution is one of accepting faults and blazing a humanitarian trail. Thus, if Atlantean energy is part of an individual's makeup, the solution to neutralizing the negativity associated with failure is complete humanitarianism. We have not observed this result in many on the planet at this time.

Does Atlantis still exist?

Being that all that ever existed in the past, present, and future continues to exist on some level, although not available for 3-D viewers, Atlantis, or the energy and vision of Atlantis and its civilization, exists in an alternate dimension that will affect those who are connected to that essence.

Transcendence

Is it possible to transcend the challenging and emotionally wrenching dramas associated with polarities?

Your Soul is a complex organism that responds and prompts you to continue your journey regardless of whether you consistently align with the highest aspects of yourself. Being open to transcending your current version of reality and allowing new ideas to permeate your consciousness will create an environment conducive to growth. All consciousness is in a void state until triggered by these awarenesses. We understand your need to grasp the unknowable. It is not a large task—it is an impossible task.

All Beings are regarded in high esteem despite behavior because they are a product of an imperfect environment. If you reject aspects of yourself, you disconnect from unity or oneness.

Prepare now to exist at a new level of awareness where you will combine your purpose with your desire to live in the heart. Go into your heart to find a gift not only of love but also of decision—a decision not to focus on what you lack, your perception of inadequacy, but on the essence of your Being. Your personal gifts transcend the 3-D version of reality but are inclusive of the quality of life you have chosen to lead. Hold the focus and intention to stay in this space.

This awakening to new versions of yourself will allow you to unzip your personas and acknowledge the diversity of your existence. Embrace your individuality and the wisdom that you have gathered to reach this stage of your existence, knowing that you are stepping onto a new stage. The unknown welcomes, embraces, and encourages you to step without fear into this next dimension of existence. You are capable of transcending the virtual reality created by mass consciousness.

Hold the vision of rising above the fray.

CHAPTER SIX:
New Perspectives for Conscious Living

Inspired to continue exploring the Universal questions and viewing my life from a different perspective, my questions continued. In the following messages, you'll learn that, although the original human blueprint has limited us, we now have the opportunity to expand our consciousness.

What is the role of the subconscious? What is the value of being mindful, living from the heart, and maintaining balance? These replies enhanced my understanding and challenged me to embody new paradigms.

Defining Your Life in New Terms

How can I maximize my ability to function and evolve beyond my current capacity to understand the nature of existence?

The life that you lead in consciousness is a trauma-related story designed to give you certain experiences. You are triggered by levels of trauma designed to allow you to respond and interact in a way that develops your consciousness. Those experiences define who you are in this lifetime. However, there is a Greater Plan that affirms your ongoing presence as an entity unto itself. You are a Soul on a journey and have had, and will have, an infinite number of experiences. When you view your life from your present you do so with an outlook only impressed with what you hold in consciousness. However, the energy of the future is calling you to define your life in new terms.

We say to you, unlock the carrier of the present and allow yourself to view the forest, then the planets, then the Universe, as holding a treasure that allows you to experience all aspects of this Being and more of yourself than you previously imagined. You are an aspect of a Greater Being and the connection to your Higher Self, as well as multidimensional strings, influences you in a way that cannot be explained to earthly consciousness. It would not be understandable at this time. Just retain this information and continue to know that there is more to life than is experienced in the third dimension. You are on a journey of discovery, ever unfolding, ever unwinding, and there is a destiny for all creatures on the planet and in the Universe that defies comprehension.

Are we being released from the original human blueprint that has limited our ability to fully comprehend the nature of reality?

Your original blueprint provides for a minimal extension of consciousness along predetermined lines. Your consciousness participates in a multidimensional drama that holds you in place to interact with the mass consciousness and those individuals whose identities match yours. Participation in this mass drama runs a current of energy throughout many frequencies.

However, a shift in the planetary alignment and a nurturing of DNA has allowed certain individuals to expand. You can choose to disconnect, or detach, from the mass frequencies. The more you question the purpose, the plan, and the reasons behind your existence, the more you will turn the mirror of your life onto a new axis. This will allow you to see beyond the illusionary 3-D reality that the masses experience.

Ask to see beyond the illusion and to understand the plan. Be open to your perceptions and energetic connections. Above all, be open to opportunities to follow signs, clues, and new insights. There will be minimal stability going forward. Ride the energetic magic carpet and open to your visions to maximize your potential.

The Subconscious

I was a single student living in Boston when I had a vivid dream. I was lying on an operating table and the doctor said, "It's a boy and a girl—what do you want to name them?" When I awoke I thought that it was a very strange dream and forgot all about it until years later when, in my ninth month of pregnancy, a sonogram showed that I was carrying twins: a boy and a girl.

How does the subconscious become conscious and how do we benefit from that?

A weed in the desert is still a weed, and yet it is an organization of environmental perfection that reached the fruition of concerted effort to thrive when there was no control.

An individual may only see the forest, while the trees are connected to the plan for the organization of that forest. When we allow all to grow together, they manage a creation of greater organization and more strength. Thus, the subconscious grows a plan for the forest by planting the seed for the first tree. You may never see the completion of this creation or you may watch it grow.

The subconscious plants the seed and the beginning of the organization of what will come to fruition is in alignment with all pieces of the puzzle.

Our subconscious agreement is that the function of life is to nurture and participate in the Divine Plan. The organization of that plan is pieced together in keeping with the highest interests of the greater Universal pulse.

Thus, the subconscious functions as a deep well that nurtures the seedlings of the Soul's Greater Plan.

Focus on Perpetual Creation

I've spent countless hours thinking about how to manipulate outcomes to get what I want and now realize that I've been resisting what I didn't want instead of embracing what I want. When I released my desires instead of trying to control the direction of the path, it ultimately resulted in a better resolution than I could have expected.

The pivot of a synchronicitous manner of living becomes more fragile with a focus on what is not right or what could go wrong. A focus on perpetual creation and magical qualities of existence moves your consciousness to a new level of awareness.

Awareness is a relative factor, depending upon a conscious wave of mass movement and trends. Trends focus on creation, or birth of new ideas, and retribution for actions taken against natural sources. By this we mean that those who have crossed over the balance or tipped the balance toward negative actions against humanity will receive retribution—a message of Universal threat. They are in a position to receive a reminder of mortality and consequences of actions not in keeping with Universal laws.

Where we keep these balances unchecked the danger of continuing to tip toward catastrophe will occur. We are in accordance with vigilance and allowing human nature to create with full disclosure of free will. However, free will has boundaries and limits.

Does this mean that action will be taken to prevent catastrophic tipping? If so, who or what will be taking these actions?

The involvement of Universal force depends upon the prevalent nature of the actions taken and where they have been taken. We regard these phenomena as outside the spectrum of human consciousness at this time. However, there is a balance that is enforced via Universal law and this is a factor of value that should be brought to your awareness.

Self Improvement

What qualities are the most important for us to develop? What are the most advantageous for our spiritual growth?

When you allow yourself some time for introspection and reflection, particular issues may come to the surface and you may identify personal aspects or qualities that you would like to improve. Self-judgment is a result of your ability to understand and consider the moral and ethical nature of your actions, and you may then make decisions regarding how you would like to behave in the future rather than how you behaved in the past.

Your emotional baggage is reflected in your interactions and may trigger a desire to change or improve your ability to interact with others and how you feel about yourself. Noticing that you do not feel satisfied about how an interaction occurred or how your life is progressing is an exceptional quality in itself because it propels you forward with the intention of self-improvement.

There is no judgment if you have trouble modifying your behavior or way of thinking. However, when you reflect on and consider those qualities that you would like to improve or interactions that inspire you to improvement and carry that with you, this reflection infiltrates your consciousness and assists you in evolving toward a more improved version of yourself.

Taking it a step further, we assure you that you are being assisted in your evolution and we are inspired to assist humanity in transitioning to another level of existence that will allow individuals to more easily release negative qualities and create the best possible version of themselves.

Living from the Heart

Is living from the heart the key to our journey to full consciousness?

When you live from the heart, your journey connects to the core nature of your Being and its desire to expand beyond the boundaries of 3-D existence. The heart knows and contains the cellular memory of existences beyond the present and into the past and future. The cellular memory identifies and reaches to those experiences most needed for you to venture into and absorb so that your consciousness understands how you are related to the Divine Plan. Simply be open to controlling your need to listen to the ego and allow the heart to speak to you.

How do I identify when it's the ego speaking rather than my heart?

Your ego speaks in "I" statements and the desires it identifies are also I-centered. The heart speaks with positive emotion, love, and caring feelings and does not require material identification. Rather, it facilitates energetic expansion.

Maintaining Balance

Is there a way for us to stay healthy on this planet?

The avenue to staying healthy depends not just on physical but also mental and emotional balance. All aspects of health are affected when an individual dives off the deep end emotionally.

The human system balances on an average of once a day. Otherwise, it is bending to outside energies, static, sunspots, and planetary influences. Thus, the first question to ask is how to maintain balance when bombarded by outside influences.

Acknowledging that outside forces will influence you regardless of your attempts to stay in balance moves your consciousness up a notch. Notice how you feel, take the temperature of your emotional state, and if feeling in balance, keep it as a yardstick for measurement.

Make a mental note that you will consciously check in to your emotional state a few times a day. If you notice that you are not in balance, stop and pull out the yardstick. Focus and see if you can move yourself back to the base line. The more you do this the easier it will become.

Also, monitor the amount of outside influences you allow into your space on a daily basis. Where is it said that the T.V. or radio should be turned on? Where is it said that you should read the news or find out what is going on in a foreign country? It was not so long ago that there was no such thing as T.V., radio, and international news. People focused on what was in front of them and the very thing they needed to do in that moment or day. Consider doing that as an exercise for a day and notice how much more balanced you feel, how much more you accomplish, and how expansive you feel.

Practice this short exercise: With your hand on your chest, imagine pushing out from your insides to the outer edge of your body and mentally create a barrier of light around yourself. As the day goes on, notice if you find that you are feeling negative for no apparent reason. If so, re-establish your light barrier and brush off the negativity.

Your very desire to remain in balance affects the fulcrum of the pendulum.

CHAPTER SEVEN:
Spanning Lifetimes, Breaking Boundaries

I had far-reaching metaphysical questions regarding topics like whether time is speeding up, the future of humanity, and if there is a part of us that knows when we're going to die. Since I believe in reincarnation, I also wanted to know whether it would be possible to bring the knowledge that I've acquired up until now into my next lifetime instead of having to begin again with a clean slate all over again.

In follow-up to the message about predestination, I was challenged to consider that there could be no judgment of human behavior even when it's perceived as wrong or bad.

The Spiral of Life

I'm beginning to understand that the perfection in nature extends to everything in our world and I've heard the term Spiral of Life used in this context. Please explain the Spiral of Life.

Perfection is a real aspect of evolution and creates the Spiral of Life as we know it. Where your evolution begins and ends is an elusive moment in time and all who seek it will be prepared to contemplate the deepest mysteries of the Universe. The Spiral returns again and again in synchronicity with your place in the moment and the Universal Cycle begins again.

Time Speeding Up

What energies are affecting us right now and how can we best handle them?

We are in a time of great change and the energies are swirling in a configuration of dimensional shift. This dimensional shift is geometrically opposed to most humans' current energy configuration, which means that it is supporting a trend toward unusual and unconventional thinking.

A perception of time speeding up is correct in that there is an acceleration of individuals who are sensing a quickening of their purpose regardless of conscious intention. Thus, when a person believes they are making a conscious decision to change they are actually being influenced by Universal force to direct their energies toward a more meaningful lifestyle arrangement. That new lifestyle will support receptive persons in using the energies of cosmic performance.

All people on the planet are experiencing reactions to the energetic shift. However, those more sensitive to energies and more elevated in consciousness will respond with action, while those who are not in sync will be further influenced to change but express negative resistance before their personal shift.

All will shift and all are being guided. Make an intention to lift the veil while in a place of decision so that those who guide, and with best intentions provide you with loving support, will be more available to you. Allow your guides to open the portal to the new energy and guide you through without resistance. As you do so the quality of the shift will be personally rewarding and satisfying.

What can you tell us about the future of humanity?

Regardless of where you are located, whether you are on the Earth or in the stars, your path is realigned frequently depending upon outside influences and choices made. However, as mentioned in previous messages, all have a predestined path, or delineated cycle of growth, that is in alignment with cosmic circumstances. At this time, the cosmic status of humans on Earth is that of walking a tightrope for no individual is immune to the toxic circumstances of their environment.

Those who believe in reincarnation know that even if life on the planet is terminated, the Souls currently assigned to it will be allocated to new bodies, regardless of the type of body or the location. Yes, you too may live among the stars, but your consciousness will also be realigned in keeping with your path.

You have reason to be concerned about the state of humanity at this time. The carriers of light on the planet, who are conscious of the dire circumstances associated with environmental risks and toxic actions taken by individuals, are not alone capable of averting potential disaster. We ask you to be vigilant to opportunities to make a difference in the lives of others, to convey your message of

Monti Scribner

life as you know it, regardless of judgmental feedback, and to hold love and gratitude in your heart for all that now exists. The vibrational frequencies associated with good actions make more of a difference than you know.

Our Potential

Is there a way to analyze a situation from the perspective of our personal history and the impact that decisions we make now will have on our future?

Yes, this is something you can allow yourself to practice and achieve in good time. All individuals have the ability to evolve into multidimensional, multisensory Beings who possess layered thought.

Access to your complete life library, past, present, and future, is available for review when requested in a way that will access only that piece of information relevant to the question. The vast amount of information available restricts access to a particular inquiry. Asking with discernment and relevance brings forth the information that can be reviewed and evaluated for assistance in making a decision. This multifaceted review of a situation is desired for an objective viewpoint. However, even if an individual is emotionally invested in the outcome it will not affect this type of review because only facts and actual experiences are presented. Akashic record readers can only deliver that amount of information that is requested and that the individual is prepared to receive at the time of inquiry.

If Akashic record readers have the ability to access an

individual's library, how is achieving the ability you describe different from that?

Your version of reality only allows individuals to perceive their lives in a particular way. There are filters overlaid upon communication based upon levels of understanding and the influence of mass consciousness.

Thus, when an individual asks a question of the Akashic records these filters influence their question and their understanding of the answer.

Steps can be taken to remove the filters so that you may ask more relevant questions and perceive answers in a layered fashion, which is more useful to decision-making.

Please explain what you mean by "layered fashion."

When individuals perceive an experience in 3-D they only view their interactions along with their emotional attachments. When they perceive in layered fashion it becomes a multidimensional experience where they perceive the cords associated with the interactions, how decisions made will affect them and those involved, how the history of associated relationships led to the interaction, and the repercussions of present actions on future events. There is also a mass consciousness ripple associated with interactions, decisions, and thought processes.

When Nothing Is Happening

It's been quite a while since I've received any messages. Why haven't I received any insights or messages recently?

When you arrive at a plateau of energy it is a resting place that allows you to survey the landscape of your life. As you do so you may reach the conclusion that nothing is happening and your life appears to be meaningless. This is not the case.

The carrier of your Soul is a thriving, ever-changing organism connected to the Universe and the Universal pulse, which ebbs and flows according to a Greater Plan. There is also a connection to intergalactic intelligence, which provides a download of frequency and information during these times when nothing seems to be happening.

Rest in the knowledge that, although you perceive that nothing is happening, there is a conveyance of knowledge and information frequency that is preparing you for the next step in your evolution. Again, there is always something happening with regard to your existence.

Parallel Lives

I've read that, as multidimensional Beings, there are other versions of us existing in other dimensions. If it's true that we are simultaneously experiencing parallel lives, how can we understand and relate to those lives in a constructive manner?

You have speculated for some time about parallel lives and soon there will be a crossover.

First, focus on an aspect of your personality that may reflect back to you as a possible polarity such as shy versus assertive. Next, think about another life that you may have led if you had chosen a different path.

Then, consider the idea of a convertible life in which your personality has different polar characteristics and yet is still recognizable. Your parallel life can also reflect back to you across generations because it has existed in that fashion.

The next barrier to cross is that of experiencing yourself inhabiting a body that coexists with your energy type, has freedom to act as you see fit, and contains a different brain pattern that allows you to create a different reality while continuing to serve your Soul's purpose. You are she and she is you.

Now begins the process. First, step into your imagination and sense this person that images you across dimensions. Reach out in your imagination and acknowledge them. Gradually, over days, continue to acknowledge and relate to them, sensing their energy and spirit as compatible with yours.

In the future, the two of you will merge to create a more powerful and relevant version of you. But for now just place your attention on this version of you and notice how it makes you feel.

Crossing Lifetimes

In a past life reading, I was told that I had been a Welsh author and metaphysical poet who lived in the 1600s. When I researched his life, there were amazing similarities between his interests and mine.

Your lives carry the vibration of past life experiences regardless of conscious awareness. Thus, focusing on the positive aspects of your current experiences and allowing them to permeate the essence of your Being will contribute to an insightful future life.

You can draw on the sensory nature of your current existence to connect with past and future lives. These experiences will overlap and blend when you allow your consciousness to open to the possibility of your greatness.

The essence of who you are is far greater than the individual encapsulated in your body.

Express gratitude to your body for being the vehicle for your Soul's expression. The programs you carry in this lifetime require you to expend a certain amount of energy devoted to the Divine Plan. However, the essence of your Soul is a vehicle for translation through all lifetimes.

Consider the notion that what you perceive as limited time on Earth, a mere blink of an eye, is actually a reflection of life's transcendence over individualization. The so-called individual personality carries the essence, or flavor, of a far larger and more expansive Being.

Open your heart to this concept and allow it to permeate your Being. Your expansion will be enhanced by this realization of transcendence.

Breaking Through Boundaries

Can we break through boundaries that limit our perceptions?

Your consciousness creates a circular path to your destination that permeates the third dimensional existence and promulgates a structure that you view as real. In fact, it is a complex construction of current events, future possibilities, and combined consciousness.

When you focus on your desires you hold in place the perspective of how you view your reality and what you want. However, this restricts you to a timeline that is unavailable and unrealistic. The constricted version of truth that you perceive is where you err in visualization. In fact, the truth is beyond your ability to perceive and the version of reality that you view is protecting you from the nature of a larger vision that is not ready for viewing.

The restricted boundaries of your perceptions are held in place by a veil that allows only those with expanded abilities to access the truth. However, the promise of a new version of human capacity will open this vista to those ready for the leap.

Such is the human imagination that many individuals can conceive of this new reality, but their focus is warped and unreliable. There are many versions of suppositions and imaginative creations regarding the nature of the Universe and how humans are controlled.

We say to you, be of yourself and perceive the truth of your own Being, which is what you know in present time. What you sense is true for you is your center and space of grounding. The security of your nervous system requires restrained use of expansion to assure that the complexity of your existence is not imploded.

Our consideration of your sensitivity, current abilities, and potential requires a slow but steady consistency in advancing your Being, pacing information so that what is given may be properly absorbed.

We want you to know that you are cared for infinitely, and the structure of your Being is connected like scaffolding to the ever-expanding Universe.

The Relationship of Time to Experiences

Please explain how the construct of time relates to our perception of reality.

Focusing on the factor of the relationship of time to your experiences invents a boundary that restricts your conscious intention and carries you along a certain defined path. However, this restriction of consciousness is capable of being reshaped and permeated by constructive use of imagination.

Imagine a circle with you in the middle and around you are all of your life experiences from birth to death. Because these experiences circle you, they can continue to circulate indefinitely. A calendar has been identified for defining your life events where you manage associations between your life path and the circumstances created.

You are now being given the opportunity to use your intention to focus outside the circle. Imagine that malleable light, which invented your circle, is available to change those experiences that appeared permanent. Also, there are parallel circles carrying different, but related, life experiences just outside your point of view.

Imagine the possibility of breaking through the boundaries; this is all you need to do at this time.

Can you give me more information about this exercise, imagining that malleable light can change those experiences that appeared permanent?

Consider changing your focus from manifesting the conscious creation of desires to becoming a light-filled, luminous Being that merges with Universal flow. When you open to the magic of the unknown and acknowledge that this guides every aspect of your life you embrace the changing mystery of existence.

Notice with your inner eye that there is no solidity to your Being but that you are made of light and part of nature. Imagine that you are merging with the Universal grid and notice where this takes you. Can you move among the angels? Your ability to see and sense these next steps requires letting go of focus on the present 3-D existence and opening to embodying the carrier of light that you are. Hence the term light worker.

Search for Destiny

What does destiny mean to an individual living on Earth today?

All possible paths lead to a destiny predetermined by life itself. Destiny provides a marker that allows individuals to progress when a quest for clarity prompts them to persist in contemplating their futures. There are no parameters for how long individuals must proceed on their path in order to reach a destiny determined by Soul essence. The Soul is an eternal quality that abides within and around individuals and is specific to their role in the ongoing circumstances of nature.

The Soul requires only that individuals exist on their particular plane of creation, and the movement in concert with destiny is not in fact a movement so much as a scattering of stars within the constellation of a firmament of eternal existence.

Climbing a stairway to a particular destination is a figment of imagination created to combine the need to understand with need to obey rules created by those who would control humanity. There are no rules, other than continued expansion in the elements of fire, air, water, earth, and knowing a sense of accomplishment that comes from following your particular path to a State of Grace.

Predestination

When I think back to some of the crossroads in my life where I was compelled to make significant decisions about the path I would take, I often wish that I had made different choices.

Think back to one of those times and imagine that you are beginning to walk down the alternate path. You will soon realize that you were not conscious enough, emotionally strong enough, and you generally did not have sufficient self-knowledge to follow that path. Also, everything that contributed to bringing you to the crossroads supported you in making the choice that you did.

The alternate path was not supported by your mental and physical condition at that time. If you could go back, even with self-doubt, you would have again chosen the same path.

Are the choices we make predestined?
Certain experiences that you have are predestined. You are engineered to create these experiences for the integration into the Whole of planetary development. You are given clues, or subtle interactions, that lead you in a particular direction.

Your inner knowing and Higher Self also guide you towards these experiences and aha moments where you realize that something is right.

The predestination of the species applies to all. All must know that there is a Greater Plan of which they are a part, and regardless of belief that plan includes decision making that they previously believed was of free will.

Your vision for your future is a conscious determination based upon past experience and insights. However, what you desire is a biological function. You own it, you experience it, and you follow the guidance provided for you.

As you do, your life will flow smoothly and easily. Follow the guideposts and the insights; stay true to your Self, and your path will unfold before you with guidance, synchronicities, and unexpected joy.

Judging Behavior

It's clear that we hinder our personal growth by clinging to old, negative issues and patterns. Do we also hinder ourselves by judging others?

When you fully understand the concept of predestination you will come to the conclusion that you can no longer judge the behavior and choices of others. You have been trained to develop preconceived ideas and to draw certain conclusions regarding your perceptions of persons or situations. But now there can be no judgment.

Even where there is destruction or violence, there is a biological function gone awry that is also compliant with an alternate plan.

All individuals require fine-tuning since none exist in a state of perfection. The idea that individuals should conform to one type of behavior is counter to the current brain formation. Thus, those who believe they have free will are actually in compliance with their biological function. Some functions also employ or create habits and psychological quirks. This has been infused through generations and tampered with via DNA.

Again, all individuals participate in a predestined life

path. Behavior appearing deviant is a biological crisis, and unfortunately, cannot be easily reframed.

Planetary oversight and re-engineering is the only possible solution to destructive deviations. However, many contributing factors must be aligned before amendments to human behavior can be made.

Beyond the Veil

Why is there a veil that keeps us from seeing true reality?

Perceptions on Earth are illusory due to the mask, or cloud, beyond which most cannot see or perceive. The 3-D experience includes a veil so that humans can function and exist on the Earth plane. Without it, there are no permanent lessons. But now, due to DNA code activation and consciousness expansion, more humans are seeing beyond the veil and thinking outside the box. They have become aware of the illusionary belief that there is a structure of solidity when there is only a web of interconnected energetic fibers and channels through which all interact in predestined experiences.

This new level of conscious awareness also affects behavior. It motivates people to express themselves with increased confidence without limiting their truth. As people become comfortable with their new identity, they experience more synchronicities and allow themselves to respond positively to the promptings of their Higher Self.

The Completion of a Lifetime

Is there a part of us that knows when we're going to die?

The completion of a lifetime includes the aspects of all

ingredients that contributed to your existence. Thus, the culmination of a lifetime is a certainty that never fails to manifest in Divine Order.

Those who contemplate the certitude of death may wonder why they lived at all and ponder when the winding road to physical extinction may culminate in that transition. However, contemplating death provides the framework for a conscious life in order to create the motivation for meaningfulness.

There are no exclusions, for the infinite nature of the Universe is characterized by the ephemeral nature of physical form. Thus, consciousness rides on the form for a short period of time and then extinction provides for expansion of divinity within the Universal force.

Those who are engineered to think outside the box and whose consciousness is designed to pioneer the next spiritual frontier for those who follow are aware that the meaningfulness of their lives hinges on a solid base of spirituality.

In answer to the question, "Is there a part of us that knows when we are going to die?" you may also ask if your death will have meaning beyond the scope of making a contribution to the Universal force. In fact, the ephemeral nature of existence relies on the birth and death of energy and the contributions of your form and consciousness propel the Master Plan.

Again, your physical existence hinges on the continual expansion of the Universe and is part of the Master Plan. Your form will terminate at the exact moment when the contribution of your cellular energy, a conscious aspect of yourself, completes its physical participation in the dance of life and merges with the Divine nature of infinite existence.

CHAPTER EIGHT:
Our Next Truth

I continued to ask questions about our changing reality, the new paradigms that are being introduced, and how to maintain balance when experiencing chaos.

What Is Our Next Truth?

- You are being guided and supported by unseen intelligences.
- The 3-D reality you focus on is a myth.
- The multidimensionality of your existence precludes control by outside forces.
- The fear that holds you is an illusion.

Once you free yourself, you may serve as a role model to enlighten others. The things that you love and value will not be lost and can remain with you as long as you desire.

Is it possible to carry consciousness into subsequent lifetimes or dimensions? If so, how?

This desire is understandable, as you wish to avoid experiencing struggles similar to those suffered up to this point in your life. However, it is better to ask how to navigate the turbulent waters of Soul experiences so as not to suffer.

The gratitude felt which transitions to a State of Grace is the vehicle to carry a Soul to the next lifetime experience with cognition.

This cognition translates as an inner knowing with the ability to glide or ride the waves of experience as if in a gently-rocking boat on an energetic ocean. It may also be experienced as a supportive multisensory state that feels like energetic silk.

As you master the ability to achieve a State of Grace in this lifetime, you will carry it to the next.

Not Immortal, But Eternal

How do we reconcile the finite nature of our lives that are often threaded with violence, turmoil, and tragedy with our desire to love and be loved so we can create a peaceful, harmonious existence?

When you ask for the reasons behind the violence and tragedy you question the bilateral nature of polarity. There is a polarity to nature that is expressed and mirrored in all that you view. Try to view the polarities as a mirror of three-dimensionality and sometimes one-dimensionality. Then, imagine walking through the mirror to view a version that may allow you to comprehend the conditions for a particular experience. From this, you may understand that there is a basis to your existence that requires these experiences to be perceived in a certain manner and creates the conditions for spiritual growth. The fifth-dimensional version of reality is not in synchronicity with this one because it is viewed from the perspective of neutral light Beings.

When you focus on intentionally merging with the eternal nature of existence you create the conditions for a new reality in which your nature is one with all. Because of the continual expansion of existence, the view of reality shifts on a minute-to-minute basis. Once you consider the spiritual growth and relative maturity of humans on the planet you will note many versions of consciousness and understanding. In fact, the kaleidoscope of consciousness is ever expanding and changing as it reacts to Universal influences.

The longing to be immortal and impervious to human conditions is frequently presented in books and movies. What does this tell us about our society? Is there a way we can use this knowledge when it comes to our attention?

This knowledge brings your attention to the fact that many believe this civilization is beyond repair and can only be restored by those with superpowers.

What has a civilization become that would require superpowers to overcome the evils of society? These stories exaggerate the characteristics of heroes; they create an ideal in which miracle workers free those who are subject to unreasonable control. So, in order to free yourselves from villains, you believe you require a savior or superhero.

But you are your own saviors and superheroes. View yourself as not subject to controlling forces but as capable of freeing yourself by manifesting personal power, expanding your multidimensional self, and connecting with your Soul.

Our Pioneering Spirit

It appears that people are evolving faster now. For instance, there are more people opening up to channel and expressing Universal concepts at a higher level. What is this about?

The DNA code gates are opening for a particular species of human whose genetic materials contain the chemistry associated with Lyra, or pioneering spirit. Those carriers of genetic codes that allow them to receive species enhancement are now opening up to understand and express their complex nature. Allowing the opening and acknowledging that you are more than you appear, that you are connected to star species outside of your 3-D reality, and that the vision of humanity's future lies outside the confines of the current star system is still experienced by very few on Earth. The Earthbound, whose codes have not been activated, will continue to function as if nothing is happening. Their consciousness is unable to open sufficiently to receive and process this information.

The galactic heritage of humans allows certain species to open to a connection with their ancestors and understand that they are associated with another family outside of their physical reality, and they are capable of connecting with that family, which serves as a support system and consciousness link. The more the DNA codes are exercised, the more their gateways open. Any fear or resistance associated with this experience will compress the communication and may eventually shut the gateway down.

When your codes are activated, you experience the part of your hologram that triggers your consciousness for further expansion. And those individuals whose codes are not yet activated will not be magnetized to a similar experience or comprehend the meaning, which will result in their neutral response when exposed to information outside of their scope.

Since the Universe is a cohesive whole containing all elements of cosmic unity, even those who do not appear to find their way are experiencing an alternate reality that balances or offsets the union or reunion of all parts. Thus, the counterbalance disconnection is as important as the expression of connection.

CHAPTER NINE:
Heart Connections

These messages offer a deeper understanding of the impact that heart-centered practices can have on maintaining emotional stability and elevating consciousness. You'll read that the practice of expressing gratitude can have far-reaching effects and that when we surrender to the human experience we open the door to the Realm of Possibilities.

Gratitude and Grace

Gratitude is a life force that exists as a separate entity, supporting the human system. It can lead to a particular State of Grace that allows a Soul to exist in a bubble of purity when the Soul's intent is exclusive of ego and has no regard for personal gain.

In gratitude the heart opens to fortunate circumstance, which serves as an armament against negativity, supplementing your energy grid and fortifying your spirit. Once a Soul achieves the State of Grace, it does not allow for negative interference.

You can manage your will and stabilize your thought

processes by creating this State with heart-centered practice, focus, and pure intention.

Surrender

The exercise of love is to be found in the heart, but the exercise of allowing is in the full body.

Release the fears and anxieties held in the body and the realm of possibilities enters for an adventure.

Surrender to the forces of nature, allowing yourself to feel the effects of the energetic promise of All That Is. It swirls like a whirlpool of stars, brightening your path.

Imagine that the stars are circling around you and lighting your way. Release the doubts and resistance to the possibility that you may create magic, because you do with every step you take, when you allow the mystical to guide you.

Step into the realm of possibilities and release judgment.

The State of Bliss

Bliss is being in concert with the Universal force and the nature of your Being, which is pure love.

The overlays of emotional stress, negative interactions, and energetic bombardment can decimate an otherwise balanced Being.

Imagine you are alone in a serene environment surrounded by trees. Sense the nature of the trees as strong, supportive, and in harmony with the Earth. Notice that each tree has a personality and its own loving heart.

Breathe in the feeling associated with being completely nurtured by your environment.

Notice how long you can hold that feeling.

CHAPTER TEN:
Some Assembly Required

As we follow our inner guidance, we are integrating the new paradigms, releasing expectations and judgments, and walking our spiritual paths. We've learned that we are uniquely equipped for this human experience. The training wheels are off and the puzzle pieces are fitting together.

Puzzle Pieces

Can you provide any other advice for individuals who are consciously walking their spiritual path?

The pieces of the puzzle continue to come together for seekers ready for next steps. Uploading unwanted aspects and downloading new parts of your psyche alleviate personal limitations. This brings in a portion of the Universal mindset that influences consciousness expansion.

The more you recognize and release old programming, the more available you are to receive upgraded elements of consciousness.

Pieces will not integrate unless compatibility is established. This also explains the differences in understanding between seekers. Individuals may not have the ability to agree because their levels of understanding depend upon the nature of their consciousness.

Regardless of differences, expanding your consciousness is not a competition. It is, however, integral to the continuing evolution associated with Universal expansion.

Expansion can happen naturally over time and individuals can actively work on elevating consciousness by healing emotionally-charged issues that interfere with their ability to achieve non-polarized thought.

An individual's denial of the existence of metaphysical concepts is also an element of consciousness associated with evolution and not to be judged.

No Expectations

It is a continuing challenge to trust that I'm being guided and that all of my experiences are in Divine Order.

Value the life you lead without expectations; it just is, and there are no promises of cause and effect. The purpose or value of experiencing polarity is recognizing your desire and then being in the energy or expectation of manifestation. Be aware that a kernel of fear about not realizing your goal may turn into dread of failure. Be in the energy of creation and every effort will develop as it should.

The completion of a lifetime includes the aspects of all ingredients that contributed to your existence. Thus, the culmination of a lifetime is a certainty that never fails to manifest in Divine Order.

Some Assembly Required

Our bodies speak to us on multiple levels and translate our experiences to enhance our connection with the Universe.

Today, give yourself permission to live fully in your body.

The feelings, senses, and emotions you receive are signals for personal actualization. Allowing yourself to not only feel, but to also acknowledge those feelings, gives your body permission to continue communicating with you.

Allow yourself to be grounded in conscious awareness (are you awake?) and gift your body with gratitude. Do things for yourself that support your immune system, physical, and emotional health.

If you exclude the physical from your daily experience you lose a piece of the puzzle of life.

The puzzle pieces are yours to assemble.

CHAPTER ELEVEN:
Visualizations

When you allow your imagination to reach for aspects of yourself that exist outside of the 3-D experience, you become open to different perspectives. These uplifting visualizations assist in making multidimensional connections.

Angel Wings Visualization

The actual nature of existence is far from what any human can conceive of. You can consider it a fanciful dance with a rearranged reality.

This is why the mention of angel wings may be viewed as fanciful fiction rather than based in reality. An introduction to your consciousness must be derived by crafting a story, or a visualization, to guide you to this experience.

Start by allowing yourself to imagine a tree full of colorful blooms growing in front of you. This is not an ordinary tree. It grows and manifests the lifestyle you perceive as yours. It uncovers the locks and keys behind your nature. It embodies your Soul and personifies your identity.

Since this tree represents your identity, the manner of

its existence is multidimensional. Focus on the center of the tree, and as you gaze at it imagine that you are walking into the center of it. Now you are within the trunk of the tree and it feels warm and alive and smells of fresh, natural bark.

Close your eyes and allow the aroma to transport you to a peaceful place. Allow your imagination to take you there, and when you arrive notice that it has no material manifestation. There are no interferences. You can stretch and be without any other Being observing you.

Now turn your attention to a space in the middle of your back between your shoulder blades, and when you are ready, begin to open and spread your wings. Stretch them out as far as they will go. Sense the freedom of recognizing your identity. You are a Being of the angelic realm. There is no need to hide yourself in this place; you can be who you are without judgment.

Take your time and be in this place as long as you like. When you know you are ready, fold your wings and return to the inside of your tree. Take one last deep breath before you leave the tree and return to life as you know it.

You now have the memory of spreading your wings. Carry this memory with you as you create your new reality.

Personal Power Visualization

The excesses and stresses of daily life are orchestrated to test you and your ability to thrive and survive. Without inner strength and a knowing that who you are reflects your Soul, you will be eroded over time to merge with All That Is.

The Soul image you project is comprised of energetic coils. It is a complex combination of DNA, multiple strands of energetic resonance, and mirrors mass consciousness. The part of you that shines through this image is a strand of Soul resonance designed to continue through time, despite the vehicle that connects with it.

Being in your power means connecting with the Soul strand that resonates with multiple lifetimes and characteristics. The Soul supports your core purpose, which is an amalgam of strong current resonances. This current runs through all aspects of your identities—not just the aspect now operating on Earth.

Seeking a perspective that expands from your 3-D individuality and acknowledges your multidimensionality lifts the burden of lifedom from your psyche.

Practice visualizing the DNA strands reaching beyond your physical body and connecting with multiple aspects of your Soul identity. Notice how the strands reach beyond your understanding of practical existence and extend out into the Universe. Do you feel lighter when you do this? The physicality of your body lifts and shifts to transform into light as you make this connection.

Allow your imagination to unleash your personhood. You are more than the boundaries of a human body. You will begin to see yourself and others through new eyes.

Personal empowerment begins with this unleashing and the acknowledgment that you are free of arbitrary boundaries.

ABOUT THE AUTHOR

Monti Scribner is a spiritual teacher who is able to connect with higher guidance to provide outside-the-box perspectives on life issues. Her heartfelt mission is to assist and support others in achieving life balance, in identifying and releasing blocks to expressing their authentic nature, and in maximizing their ability to navigate life experiences more easily.

She was practicing automatic writing when she created the Formulas4Living.com blog in 2013. During her blogging experience, Monti began to ask for answers to questions that were beyond her scope of knowledge or expertise and received enlightening, unexpected answers about the nature of reality.

Monti eventually came to realize that she was accessing a higher aspect of her own consciousness that connects with interdimensional frequencies and wisdom.

The messages contained in this book, along with Monti's anecdotes and insights, offer an enlightened perspective regarding the nature of the human predicament and the value of the Earthly experience.

Monti provides client readings with a global perspective on past, present, and future. She identifies individual life lessons and karmic themes, weaving them into a framework of how life experiences contribute to Soul growth. Client sessions also include insights for solving personal problems.

Formulas4Living.com

CPSIA information can be obtained
at www.ICGtesting.com
Printed in the USA
BVOW01s0442151216
470873BV00008B/36/P